Only the Thought, of Helplessness

(A Memoir)

By: Leanora Marie Regan

1663 LIBERTY DRIVE, SUITE 200
BLOOMINGTON, INDIANA 47403
(800) 839-8640
WWW.AUTHORHOUSE.COM

First published by AuthorHouse 11/09/05

ISBN: 1-4208-4919-0 (sc)

Printed in the United States of America
Bloomington, Indiana

This book is printed on acid-free paper.

Forward

This memoir is dedicated to, "God the Father". He gave me the strength to survive my rehabilitation, and the courage to deal with the outcome. Though my abilities have changed, I am given serenity and delight by the knowledge of God's affection toward me. Any dilemma or fear I develop has crumbled the minute I reminded myself of Divine love.

During the first ten years of my life I lived without difficulties, but I don't remember how I felt back then. I'm always told, "It's a wonder you were able to make it through college," but college was just another obstacle to pass through, with a goal to reach for, whether disabled or not. My memoir was a report in college and my professors told me it should be published. Years later, after I had considered publication, I showed it to friends and saw that my life touches other people. I want as many people as possible to be inspired, and publication would spread it quickly.

Some people say to me, "You're young and you shouldn't have to go through all this," but I don't see myself as having a disadvantage from others. I can't picture my life being lived differently, I feel this is the way my life just is. I don't have the memory of a perfect life to compare with my present life, and make living now look bad. So it's a wonderful life, and to me, a normal one.

I sat up on the bed, alone in that room and thought to myself, "My life is ruined." Looking down at a blank sheet of paper, I realized turning to a person for comfort would be unrealistic, so God took that person's place. Whether there was, or wasn't a God, didn't matter. I just needed someone to provide hope. I faced the paper and began to write, not simply words, but expressions taking the place of my helplessness feelings. Phrases like, "I have so much fear" and "For it is in You that I become so strong." I didn't need to consider what I was writing, my hand just moved on the paper and I wrote a poem to God. The poem was entitled, **Oh Lord I Need Your Help.**

<u>Oh Lord I Need You Help</u>

My life is ruined
the darkness is here
Nothing goes right
I have so much fear
The good times are gone
the bad times arrived
The dangerous feelings
that beside me so long
Are making me feel
like singing a psalm
Dear God, oh my Lord
I need Your help
For it is in You
that I become so strong
To pass through life's heartaches
and to pass through life's worries
That last forever, and forever long

In Rusk rehabilitation center, I had feelings of loneliness since I missed my family and friends. I was very sad that my dog, Midnight, couldn't come visit me and extremely uncomfortable sleeping in a place different from my house. But I was able to let my feelings out with the use of a pen, because of a girl in the hospital room next to mine. Rusk Institute is the rehabilitation center of New York University Hospital (NYU). She had had one leg amputated and was learning to walk with a metal leg while in Rusk Institute. I entered her room for company, and when I got there, she was sitting on the bed with her good leg hanging off the edge. The girl, Madeline, wrote poetry and handing me an open notebook, asked me to give my opinion of her poem. She was seventeen, but to me, her poem seemed to be lacking something. I was eleven and when I read it I had my own reasons for not liking it, for example, I felt poetry should always rhyme. After reading it, I covered the breathing tube sticking out of my neck, and said to her, "I don't like it, it doesn't rhyme, I bet I could write a poem better than you."

I was in Rusk Institute after having brain surgery, which left me with partial paralysis of the body, trouble breathing and hearing, walking and learning, etc. When an eye is paralyzed and does not close, it does not tear or create moisture and can get infected. To keep my right eye from infection, a piece of gold was attached to the underside of my eyelid to weight it down. During the school year, after my hospital stay, the gold weight was removed. The eyelid had been down for a long time and lifting it needed to be worked on. When I returned to school after the operation, I wore a green patch over my eye to cover it as it healed and strengthened. When the

3

patch was gone, it took a lot of time before my eye would fully open and not squint.

My family had always told me, "You have a big mouth" and my friends would tell me I talked too much, but the breathing tube, kept me from being able to speak. I was like a television on mute, because my lips moved, but no sound came out. My dad gave me a binder of loose-leaf paper to write on so people could read whatever I tried to say. Thanks to the influence of Madeline, when I was alone, I would write poetry in that binder. Soon I began to write many more poems and my poetry became known throughout the hospital floor. The poems were mostly confined to the feelings I had while in the hospital. For example, there were poems like, **I Miss Everything** and **My Life Has Changed**.

I Miss Everything

I miss my family
and I miss my home
I miss every place
I used to roam
I miss my friends
and I miss my school
I want to learn the golden rule
I miss the life I used to live
I miss the love
I'd get, and I'd give
I miss the friendships
my friends and I made

I miss the hardships
my friends and I paid
I miss everything
I used to know
I miss everything
that made me feel low

My Life Has Changed

Though my life has changed,
not for the better
I try and make it
without feeling blue
even though, I sometimes do
Nothing goes right
and I have so much sorrow
I have no friends
and I have no plan
To get me home
as soon as I can
I've been in the hospital
a very long time
How can I say,
that it is OK?

Most of my poems were focused on my hospital stay, but after speaking with Madeline, my first poem was a gift for my mother and my father told me to title it <u>Mother's Day.</u>

Mother's Day

Mother's day comes and goes
I'm sure you do love the snow
That falls from the sky
to our heavenly earth
What made you a mother
was that you gave birth
To two beautiful children
who you'll never hurt
Because you're their mother,
now and for life
Don't ever threat to give a piece
of everlasting advice

"Rusk" looked like a hospital both from the inside and the outside, because it was connected to "Tish", the main hospital in NYU. There were many floors and each floor was extensive. The floor I was on had many rooms, but only one nurses station. Most rooms had two beds inside, and since I was in Intensive Care, my room was somewhat big. It was the room next to the nurses' station, and I'm glad, because instead of a wall there was a glass between the nurses and me. A wall at night would have created enough loneliness to shatter me. At night I had the sight of the nurses walking back and forth while doing their work, and with the comforting feeling of company beside me, I would sit up and write poetry.

I spent six months in NYU Medical Center. While I was there it felt like a few days, but as I look back on it, it seemed like a lifetime. My outlook on life changed while I was there and the whole world seemed different when

I left. Inside NYU Medical Center the days seemed to go by fast, like a flash of light. Exercises were constantly repeated, leaving time to go by quickly. In my mind, every event was happening over and over again. Many actions were similarly repeated, but the poems I wrote were always brand new. At first I wrote them for myself, but later I wrote poems for people.

I felt like I was speaking to another person as I expressed my feelings in my poetry. When I was in grade school I only wrote short poems. I was not intrigued by poetry until I reached Rusk. I was mostly inspired to write by the solitude I felt. I loved to talk and when I couldn't, writing was the type of expression I chose. The only reason I have which would influence my writing to come out in the form of poetry, is inspiration from God.

I forgot what it was like to be outside. Rusk Institute was in New York, but I never got a chance to get a headache from the noises of the city. It is said, when a person begins to do the same things everyday, the person is in a rut. My program schedule was to be woken up at seven o'clock, fed, given medicine and transferred to another room to begin treatment exercises. I wasn't bothered by the tiresome rehabilitation, because I didn't realize that I could be enjoying my time if I was at home. For a long while, I was in a wheelchair and not able to get up, I would do exercises to strengthen my hands, wrists and arms. One exercise I did for my hands and wrists was handling putty, and the exercise done for my arms was lifting weights. When the doctors decided it was time to start getting ready to walk, I did point and flex exercises with my feet and I would lift my leg up and stretch my calf. I walked while in the

Intensive Care unit of "Rusk", but in a very disorganized manner, and only from my room to the nurses station.

I was in the Intensive Care unit of "Tish" for two months, and strait from there I was transferred into "Rusk Rehabilitation Center". When I stood up for the first time in "Rusk", I saw myself as a stronger person. The focus of the therapy, before I could stand, was on my arms, but the minute I could stand the focus changed. I still worked on my arms, but the new exercises I began, concentrated on strengthening my legs. Walking did not come quite as easily as one might think. The important ingredient in walking correctly is balance, and unfortunately I had Hydrocephalus, which is caused by spinal fluid not draining correctly from the brain. Hydrocephalus creates bad balance and I stood hunched back and walked as if I were dizzy.

Before my operation I had over eight years of dance experience, and the physical therapist also happened to be a trained dancer. Ballet exercises were used, because much of the therapy was for balance. To begin re-learning how to walk, I would move forward while holding on to bars connected to the wall. Balance was very important, and it required specific exercises. One exercise I did to help my balance was trying to balance on a ball. Physical therapy is the treatment of injury by physical means, such as exercise, massage and heat, rather than drugs. The whole right side of my body was extremely weaker then the left side (including my arms and legs), and was partially paralyzed needing rehabilitation. A few months after leaving Rusk, I returned to taking dance lessons. My first and last years of dance took place in Asdal school of dance. While in the dressing room, the first time after the operation, I stood hunched back. But as I walked onto the dance floor, my eyes opened a little more and suddenly I began to stand straight. My body was saying, "This is where I've wanted to be."

I received occupational therapy too. Occupational therapy is designed to divert the mind and to correct a physical defect. There were probably even more different exercises for occupational therapy than physical therapy. One exercise was making a picture by putting together the colored wooden pieces of a puzzle. Some of occupational therapy was actually fun, I got to play word games and draw pictures.

In the room where most exercises took place there was a television. It was only on during break time from therapy, but I didn't remember the shows I liked. One morning, I had no particular television show to search for, I began flicking channels. I found a game show called Classic Concentration. In my mind, the show was wonderful, I really liked it, and every time I could watch it, I did. I didn't always have control of the television and I didn't always have a break at the time Classic Concentration was on. Every morning I would grab control of the television and make sure it got turned on to channel four, for "Classic Concentration." Eventually, the nurses allowed me to have a break at ten-thirty every morning. They considered the show as one of my occupational therapy word games and let me have complete control of the television. They thought of the show as a word game, because it started as a memory game. In it the player had to match the numbers, so the numbers would disappear. There was a picture behind the squares of numbers on the screen, and in order for more of the picture to be seen, you'd try and erase as many numbers as you could. Then you needed to try and understand the statement being made by connecting the pieces of the picture. I was good at the card game Memory and I was great at Classic Concentration. Being good at it makes me like the game more. The only reason getting control of the television was important to me was I wanted to watch "Classic Concentration".

I became friends with another patient, name Billy. He took rehabilitation especially for his upper body. He was eighteen and had dived into a pool hitting his head on the bottom. His legs became paralyzed, and he took his therapy with me. He saw how I had gotten permission to watch a specific game show every day, and he tried to get the nurses to let him watch his favorite game show too. It was called, "The Price is Right". What he didn't want to accept was his game show was an hour long and Classic Concentration was only a half-hour long. The nurses weren't going to give Billy (or anyone else) an hour break from their therapy. It was cool. I was the only patient to get special treatment by them, and it felt really good. I felt like I had the nurses wrapped around my finger.

Now I am out of Rusk and in The College of Staten Island. One day I was in the disabilities office and I met a twenty-six year old man. It was Billy. If my mother wasn't in the office with me, I never would have realized who he was. He knew me, and when I saw him I hugged him. Memories came into my head like when you find a long lost friend. I spoke to my friend, Isreal about the T. V. problem in the hospital and he said to me, "Why didn't you watch your show and then let Billy watch the last half hour of his?" I never gave thought to the great idea, and when I heard it, I felt stupid. Great idea or not, I'm glad we didn't do it, because having friends while I was there kept me mentally together and made the days much more comfortable. It felt wonderful to see Billy again, learning he never gave up and set goals for his future. I was extremely happy to see Billy in school with me and I always will be.

My mother traveled to Manhattan from Staten Island almost everyday to visit me and she always brought letters and gifts. She brought the gifts from my relatives and friends for me to see them, but when she would leave, everything she brought had to go home with her except for a few letters. People I didn't know were sending me gifts, my friends, family, friends of my family, their friends. I had churches I never heard of praying for me; people in different states, churches in different states, anyone connected to the chain of people. One gift my Great Aunt sent me was a giant stuffed animal. It was a blue and white rabbit and it was huge. I remember it in my room at Rusk, but I think of my mother wanting to carry each gift to me, though she knew she was going to have to bring the gift home. The rabbit was nearly three and a half feet tall and it meant a lot to me when my mother would bring a gift to New York to see me smile. The day I left the hospital, my mother and family carried garbage bags full of letters and gift cards out of my room and it doesn't even come close to the amount of get well presents waiting for me at home.

While I was in Rusk, my three best girlfriends from home, Melissa, Jennifer and Michelle came to visit me with my mother. It was the middle of the school year and they would inform me the gossip concerning school classmates. Patients were constantly walking in the halls with nurses and in the TV room for exercise. One of the male patients

I knew, Larry, implied he had a crush on Michelle one day that my friends came to visit me. At their next visit I told Michelle, she loved the thought of a boy liking her and she got so excited when I told her about Larry. I felt great for Michelle until she left the hospital and I saw Larry using harsh words toward another patient. When evening came I felt furious. Until that incident, I couldn't acknowledge my hospital life as being any different than the life I'd have outside the hospital. I didn't remember what it was like outside of the hospital, and I couldn't compare it to the way my life was. Concentrating on that which was happening around me, I came to realize he was annoying and had a big ego. When the lights went out,(except the lights from the nurses' station), the horrible thought of him upsetting Michelle replayed in my head. I had not stopped writing poetry at night and my horrible thoughts of him made me spend the night thinking differently about my hospital life. With him in mind, I wrote a poem entitled, **This Place is Horrid.**

This Place Is Horrid

This place is horrid
you don't know what I mean
This place is horrid
you don't know what I've seen
I hate it here,
and so would you
If you had to stay here
for a month or two
I do my best
like a bird does it's nest

To leave this place and get home
to see, my sweet mother's face

In Rusk, I spoke to a social worker who wanted to help me deal with any problems I had. One of her first questions was about what brought me to the hospital. I told her, that while I was in sixth grade, everyday I would wake up with a headache. Not a normal headache, but a headache severe enough to make it hard to stand. Every morning, I walked down the stairs in my house, with my chin up and my head turned to the right side, because holding my head up was the only way I could stand the pain. The only position able to make my headache bearable was sitting sideways on my grandmother's rocking chair with my knees curled up, my head back and my face turned to the right side. Weeks went by and the headaches consistently continued every morning. Lunchtime at my school ended by one o'clock and around twelve thirty I would finally get rid of my headache. I didn't go to school any day of the week until one o'clock in the afternoon. Having so much class time unattended, I spent my Saturday afternoons at my teacher, Mrs. Borrows's house taking tests I was missing and receiving information I wasn't being taught. The pain did finally end at twelve thirty and it was weird, because the pain would end at about the same time every day.

I informed the social worker that one day after school, I was in my room speaking to my best friend Melissa on the phone. I was having trouble hearing her and I kept switching from my right ear to my left ear in hopes of hearing Melissa better. Finally, I realized I could hear her better on the left than on the right. I asked her repeatedly, "Melissa, can you hear me better in one ear than in the other?" She kept saying, No, and I went on stating, "I don't understand." She consistently told me I was crazy and finally called out, "No, just go tell your mother!" Melissa saved my life when she told me to tell my mother, because I did tell my mom and suddenly my life changed.

My mother immediately took me to my ear doctor, Dr. Wiesenthal, because she thought I had fluid in my ear and she was happy, thinking that the fluid was the cause of my headaches. There was no fluid in my ear and Dr. Wiesenthal couldn't figure out why I was losing hearing in my right ear. He wanted to figure out what made one ears' hearing better than the other, so he scheduled me for a magnetic resonance imaging test, (MRI). The test apparently showed a brain tumor growing below my ear on the right side. The tumor had already grown to a large size. I was quickly taken out of school and put into New York University hospital, because there was not enough time to wait until summer recess since in time it would get worse. I'd be worrying about my life if I did.

Before I left school I went to speak with Miss Lucas, the fifth grade teacher. My mother had told me Miss Lucas had had a brain tumor removed. I wanted to ask her how scared I should be to have a life threatening operation. Her biggest response to me was, "You have nothing to worry about."

My tumor was the size of a grapefruit. The diagnosis given by my surgeon stated; "Fresh without solution labelled "brain tumor"are two irregular pieces of soft tantissue together 0.9 x 0.2 x 0.2 cm. They are used separately with diagnosis "Posterior fossa, excision biopsy: Neoplasm, suspicious for meningioma." Additionally, in formalin are two specimens. The first labeled "brain tumor", consists of multiple irregular pieces of soft and rubbery tan and focally dark tissue, together 3.2 x 1.8 x 1.2 cm. The second labelled "charred brain tumor" consists of four irregular pieces of firm dark tissue together, 1.2 x 0.4 cm.. The microscopic examination stated; All sections show a tumor of moderate to focally high cellularit. The tumor cells form many whorls, broad syncytial lobules, and many small microcystic areas. The tumor cells have round to ovoid or even elongated normochromatic nuclei with eosinophilic cytoplasm and ill–defined cell borders. Many psammoma bodies are seen. There are rare mitotic figures."

After my hospital stay, I returned to school on the upcoming trimester. I sought out Miss. Lucas, went up to her and said, "You lied!"

The social worker learned my operation took seventeen hours to complete and well known neurosurgeons to operate; Dr. J. Wisoff, Dr. F. Epstein and Dr. R. Abbott M.D.. I told her one of the last things I said before the operation. It was an order to my surgeon, I said, "Don't cut all my hair off." She found out I left the operating table in a coma and developed pneumonia while in the intensive care unit of Tish. She learned why I was in NYU, but wanted to know why I needed rehabilitation and how I was since I was in Rusk. I informed her the rehabilitation was for the complications caused by the surgery. Complications with breathing, walking, weakness and learning etc. I told her I felt fine and any bad feelings I had would come out at night as I wrote my poetry. I'd feel especially good as I watched people smile when I'd give them one of my poems.

While I was hospitalized my great- uncle passed away, I was very close with him. My mother asked the social worker if it would be safe and sufficient to tell me about his death. The social worker met with me and showed me the picture of a man in a hospital bed and I said to her, "Why is he in the hospital, we know he's going to die anyway?" I wish I had never said that, because I was not told of my favorite uncle's death. After I left the University hospital, I still wasn't told. Years later I began to question my little memories of a great- uncle, and though I had a remembrance of him, I was left to figure out the answer on my own. I finally realized that my great- uncle Pete died of heart problems while I was in the hospital. The social worker worked with me for two to three months, which was half of the time I was in Rusk.

After I finished working with the social worker, my life returned to it's daily medical routine. I didn't need to put aside time for a visit with the social worker. I started my day with breakfast and kept on going with therapy. I didn't eat normally, I had a stomach tube (in medical terms, a Gastro tube). My breakfast was in liquid form. A syringe would be pushed into the end of my stomach tube, and then the liquid would be poured into it. After I'd been fed, I would begin my therapy. Whenever night time came, I'd sit alone in my room and begin writing poetry. I would write, while looking at the nurses station and watching the nurses walk back and forth as they organized papers and typed on computers. The nurses made me feel like I had their company and I was comforted by their presence. Getting fed and doing my therapy took up my mornings, afternoons, evenings and nights and totally made up the time I spent in Rusk, which I consider as my hospital life. In Tisch, the hospital section, I was getting over my operation and I practically don't remember those days.

I only remember what took place in Rusk.. Tisch is not included in the recollection of my past hospital life, but everything from my time in Rusk is, though it was mostly a rehabilitation center. I was in Tisch to recover from my operations. I was in a coma and asleep most of the time while I was there.

In Rusk I was not asleep and the few memories of the hospital I've been able to keep in mind, consist of the things which took place while I was in Rusk. I remember how confused and scared I felt when five months after my operation, it was decided the trache could be removed from my neck. I was confused because I was taken into my room and laid on the bed, and I didn't understand why. I started to think I was simply waiting to be taken into an operating room. Two nurses were there with me, the nurse practitioner, Bonnie the psychologist and the doctor. Each nurse held one of my arms, the nurse practitioner took one leg, Bonnie took hold of the other. I became scared when the doctor grabbed my trache. He didn't say anything, so I wasn't sure what he was about to do. He pulled the trache up through my body and out my neck. I figured out why my arms and legs were being held down, (to save the doctor from me), because it was extremely painful and I wanted to stop him and push him away.

Rusk was not always bad, I do have nice memories of Rusk; memories of the friends I made and the poems I wrote etc. A funny memory coming to mind, is the weird obsession for ink pens I acquired. I began by collecting pens, but not using them,(which sort of treats the pens as if they were collectors' items). The reason for my obsession is, I realized the doctors and nurses pens each had the name of a medicine on them. I thought of a medical name as a funny and unusual word to show up on a pen. I wanted to save each pen to bring it out and look at it whenever I wanted to. I borrowed pens from any doctor, nurse or therapist who would let me and I usually didn't give the pen back. Sometimes I would ask the person if I could keep the pen after I was finished using it, other times I would borrow it and simply keep it. My escapade became known to most of the medical professionals in Rusk and there are eyewitnesses to the fact, people would hide their pens as soon as I was in taking distance. The escapade went on for the rest of the time I was in the University hospital. I did have an extremely large amount of pens as the collecting of pens continued. I was able to retrieve at least one pen from most people who came into contact with me. There was still one particular pen I was not able to take into possession. It was not any old pen, it was a pure gold pen which was owned by my neurologist, Dr. Allen. I saw him carrying his gold pen in the chest pocket of his suit. He always refused to let me borrow it, because he knew if I borrowed it he wouldn't get it back. I collected a lot of pens and after a while I lost empty spaces where I could put the pens I had gotten. After my treatment, I left the hospital with many garbage bags full of pens. As one of my doctors, I still see Dr. Allen. A few years after I came out of Rusk, his office was in Beth Israel Medical Center. I tried to take his golden pen,(during an appointment) he still carried it in his pocket. I never took possession of that pen and I did finally give up collecting pens, but not every doctor forgot about it. I go for a MRI six months regularly, and one day in the radiology dept. of Beth Israel Medical Center before an MRI, I saw Dr. Ziffert, a doctor I knew in NYU. When Dr. Ziffert saw me he said to the nurse next to him, "Watch out for her, this one likes pens."

While I was in the hospital, time went on and at night I would look out my window to see the lights on the Empire State Building go on and off. It was like a light from heaven giving me strength. I saw my goal as getting into the city. My mind would be concerned with missing Mass. I could not leave the hospital to go to church, but there was a hospital chapel. I was not allowed to go there either. One reason, which might have kept the nurses from bringing me to the chapel, was they felt trying to get me there would be more trouble then it was worth. There were many problems causing their decision. One was I had a trache to help me breathe, which kept me from swallowing, and therefore I couldn't take communion. They obviously didn't understand receiving communion was not the single reason for a person to attend Mass. Another problem was the chapel being upstairs and me being in a wheelchair, making it hard to get me to Mass. Maybe the biggest problem was needing my oxygen tank and suction machine carried up to the chapel too.

With everyone set against me traveling upstairs, I decided I'd try to get the nurses to change their minds. In order to do this, I began to preach to people and increase the amount of religious poetry I'd write. I wasn't becoming a nun, I was feeling close to God, and I wanted other people to. I did actually grasp people's attention, because I convinced the authorities to start having Mass, although they had stopped for a long time. I was finally taken to Mass in the hospital chapel and I got nurses to go with me. They had totally stopped going to Mass themselves until then. The nurses fixed the problems they had in the beginning that kept me from going to the chapel. They first brought me, my wheelchair and oxygen tank by way of elevator, and since I had gotten nurses to go along to the chapel with me, one of them got the idea of breaking the Eucharist into little pieces, softening the host by mixing it in water and having me receive Communion by way of my stomach tube. It had taken the nurses four months before they brought me to the chapel for Mass but I was so glad when they did. The day I went to Mass I began mentally participating in it and I felt God entered me. After going to Mass I wrote a poem.

<u>Part Of Me</u>

A long time ago if you looked into me
you'd be surprised at what you didn't see
You'd notice I had just one missing part
and the part that I craved was the true Sacred Heart
Without that one Part I would not be a whole
I needed that Part in creating my soul
The Part that was missing was the Lord God above
so I reached for His guidance and I reached for His love
When my soul got it's fill, making God part of me
I decided to try and be as He'd be
Ever since the Lord came I show without doubt
that His wishes go through me and I carry them out

Though I attended masses in my parish, after returning home from NYU, I did not receive communion. I still had the stomach tube and if I left my house, I had it twisted and taped to the side of my stomach, hidden beneath my shirt. I didn't receive the Eucharist again till after November 4th 1992 when I swallowed for the first time.

The Rosary was said every night in the recreation room and any nurse or patient who wanted could group together to pray. The Rosary is a popular devotional prayer of the Roman Catholic Church, which uses a chaplet of beads for the counting of prayers. The prayer, Hail Mary, is repeatedly announced ten times in each of five decades. A meditation of an event in the life of Christ and of the Blessed Virgin Mary are recalled before each decade and referred to as a mystery. Billy and I would repeatedly get together with the nurses and one night, the head nurse for the night shift lead the decades of the Rosary. Between two decades of the Rosary, she announced the wrong mystery and I complained, even though I could not speak, I used hand signals to infer that she was wrong, not sign language, but a kid's way of saying, "No!"

The Power Of Prayer

Brawn comes from the brain
'cause you pray with your mind
Your heart and your soul
and your spirit combined
Nothing is stronger,
than the thoughts in a prayer
The Lord's there to listen
and send you His care
The Lord hears your words
whether spoken or felt
If you ask for His help
your heartache will melt
If you praise Him with glory
you will toughen your mind

With the love that you know
He gives all humankind
Sturdy and stronger from the power of prayer
content and courage, adapting the air
The closer to God, the firmer you feel
'cause the energy from love is truly ideal

The experience I received from being in the hospital helped me to realize the true need for having a Higher Spirit in my life. The high spiritedness I was able to have, even with having disabilities, was produced by my understanding that God is part of me. By having this knowledge in my mind I felt like I had a specific power with me which produced a feeling of inner strength. I have kept these feelings with me and they help me extremely in dealing with any problems, medical or otherwise. The stronger feelings of a Divine Spirit inside me, the bigger space He would fill in my heart and it would make the space of the problem to simply feel smaller. When I know someone is there with me, constantly helping me, I am more able to handle any problems I have. Having someone love me is a great feeling, probably the best feeling there is. Knowing God is there loving me, brightens my world. From this feeling I get the courage I need. Another wonderful feeling comes by having extreme love toward someone else. Loving God keeps me content. A faith in God, is a faith in love. When I know where something is coming from, I like it better. When I look at the troubles in my life, I see they come from all over. By looking at the good things in my life and knowing they are coming from God, I like them better and I can focus on the good. Problems are produced in every life and I'm aware my hospital life was one of them, but I know God didn't make it happen. He does have the power to stop it from happening, but I understand He has extreme reasons for not stopping a problem. I like to think God's reason for not keeping me out of NYU was for my poetry. My poetry didn't blossom till I was in Rusk and because He can see the future and saw what I could give others, He let me stay there and produce poems. When I think of how my problem might lead to help someone somewhere in the future, I learn that helping God is a great gift.

Through God's Eyes

The world seems much clearer
when I look through God's eyes
I can make out the reasons
for the tears I have cried
I can understand heartache
and I understand pain
I then see that no problem
ever happened in vain
Every trouble created
has a reason to flare
It will lead to some help
to someone who's somewhere
God will be seeing
the good that it draws
And by looking through Him
pure thoughts evolve more
I can make out a concept
with the thoughts of God's ways
How He'd look upon it,
knowing how the future plays

<u>Inner Strength</u>

The sky is dark
the day is bleak
Boredom fills me
and so I feel weak
But I'm able to stand
for I've strength deep inside
A power within me
from which I can't hide
The Key of my soul
fits the door of my life
And with Him as a comfort
I won't fill with strife
I can withstand my enemies
for I'm never alone
'Cause it may not be known
but the Lord's in my bone

My brother, Michael, was graduating St. Margaret Mary elementary school on June 13th and I was released from the hospital one week beforehand. Before leaving the room I grabbed a remembrance. I grabbed the extra roll of toilet paper. It was like saying to myself, "Heh, it's over and I survived."As I walked through the hospital halls and down the elevators on my way to leaving, the largest thought in my mind was that the hard work was simply the pathway getting me to my goal. I attended the graduation and along with me came my private duty nurse, suction tank and oxygen tank.

When I came home there was a bed sheet stretched out on the front of my house over the door saying, "Welcome

Home Leanora!" My family, friends and neighbors were excitedly glad to see me, but I hardly saw them. I noticed the bed sheet as the ambulate door opened, but as I walked through my yard my right eye was closed and my left eye was focused on the door. I only saw people from the corners of my eye. When opening the basement door, I was shocked by the brightness of outside suddenly becoming a dark room. The windows in NYU were large and there was always light, but in my house, the window was covered by an air conditioner. I had not felt such enclosure in a long time. With an "Out of space" feeling I walked through my grandparent's bedroom and into their living room, but before I could get to the stairway, my grandmother called from behind me. My grandmother came to me carrying my favorite stuffed animal. It was a raccoon and when she gave it to me she began to laugh and explain why it had no neck. She found it in my room, thought to clean it before giving it to me, and washed it in the washing machine. While in the washer, (she didn't think to wash it by hand) it's head fell off. Thankfully, she was a retired seamstress and was able to sew the head back on. It looked sort of weird having a large head and a large body with a skinny little neck, but I was happy to see it anyway. The stuffed raccoon is kept in my bedroom, but it looks better. It has a neck brace that I made from a leg warmer used in my past ballet classes.

She showed it to me and I was happy, but I was concentrating on getting to the third floor to see my room. I went up the stairs, not turning the light on, and putting the cane on each step before me, pushing myself up and to the next step. As I climbed I was only seeing the step in front of me. When I opened the door, I suddenly saw that bright light again, because the window was open. I was just getting to the highest step when I saw my cat, Snowy Paws, sitting on the kitchen chair, then jumping up and off the chair at the sight of me. A big, "Meow" came out of her mouth and she landed in front of me. Later on, Midnight tried to bite me and I felt he forgot me, but Snowy Paws didn't. I started to like cats better than dogs. I remember the incidences vividly, and now I am a, "Crazy Cat Lady."

I walked through the dining room and up the stairs. The second flight of stairs was much easier to climb, because light came through the windows and having done it before, I faced my head up and focused on the wall at the top of the stairs.When I reached the top, I turned to my room and opened the door, it was like a picture from a story book. The first sight was the picture of a dancer on the wall straight across from the door. My family redecorated the room for my homecoming. It was organized, cleaned and repainted. My favorite color is blue. The walls, the ceiling, the frame of the window, the bed sheets and the door were all blue. My moments of being alone ended as my mother entered my room. I usually had a nurse or someone else with me afterwards.

I left the hospital with problems. Problems like; a learning disability with making mental connections, hearing loss in the right ear, on the right a paralyzed vocal chord, asthma, short-term memory loss, a G tube (Gastro stomach tube), Hydrocephalus and unending Bells palsy on the right side of my face (surgery caused paralysis). The G tube was put in March 19th., 1992 and taken out March 19th., 1993. Problems developed like; double vision with a stigmatism, epilepsy, scoliosis, a corpusloteal cyst, breathing spasms, lactose intolerance, a panic disorder, scar tissue, gastritis, a distorted brain stem, and an inoperable lesion in the brain. At this time in my life I am at the point of having had thirteen operations. I'm no longer in Rusk, but my hospital life has not ended, it just changed. A few days after coming home, I sat up on my bed alone in my bedroom and thought to myself, "It's over." I faced my binder and began to write, but this time I was writing to myself.

Again, My Life Has Changed

Again my life has changed
I am home where I should be
No more doctors, no more nurses
forever I am free
The hospital is behind me
and my life is whole again
My friendships and my hardships
have now begun to mend
All my troubles left me
and there's one thing left to see
My family helped me through it
and forget that, "No, not me!"

The poem states that in my mind there was no more to worry about. I'm glad I felt like that then, but if I wrote it at this point in my life much of this poem would need to be changed. I'd be erasing some lines, especially the line, "No more doctors, no more nurses" and, "The hospital is behind me."

The sacrament, "Anointing of the Sick", is given to those who are seriously ill. I received this sacrament three times while in the hospital. God made sure I could withstand, the challenges I'd been dealt. The Lord still does, and always will.

<u>Finding God</u>

Searching for God
and finding His trail
As if I were blind
and He was my Braille
Within my own heart
and within my own soul
Catching the Lord
has just made me whole
I knew God was in me
when first we did meet
Now I should take note
of the way my heart beats
The power He gives me
to pass through each day
Goes up and goes down
but it works either way
And now that I've met Him
I can truly say,
That the Lord is my Soul
in each and every way

Epilogue

"**Hope springs eternal,**" and the answer to living peacefully is hope. With the faith that any problem can be fixed dealing with dilemmas is much easier. Even if the problem is never corrected, having the hope that it will, prevents troublesome thoughts from entering my mind. I have hope and my outlook on life is for the future. Any inspiration I can give someone through my poetry means a great deal, and I intend on the publication of more poems.

(Psalm:23;4-6)

Yea, though I walk through the valley of the shadow of death, I will fear no evil: for Thou art with me; Thy rod and Thy staff they comfort me. Thou preparest a table before me in the presence of mine enemies: Thou anointest my head with oil; my cup runneth over.

Surely goodness and mercy shall follow me all the days of my life: and I will dwell in the house of the Lord forever.

My Serenity Prayer

I have found serenity
in accepting my cross
And I know I can bare it
'cause God's love is a force
I take strength from God's love
it drives heartache away
And gives me tranquility
in facing each day
The wisdom to realize
if a change can be made
Will come from the Lord
Who's poise can't be weighed
When there's a chance of a change
and I need courage to fight
I will look to the Lord
He will be my Light
He will strengthen my soul
with courage and care
His wisdom and love
puts peace everywhere

PART TWO

THE MODERN GOD OF LIFE

The sun begins arising
the darkness fades away
I wake up from my sleeping
it's the start of a new day
The weather changes quickly
and I face the clouds above
Then peaking out from heaven
I see God's eternal love
The rain falls down so slowly
giving water, bringing life
The fact and act of living
is God's love as strength toward strife
Then heaven shares it's beauty
as a rainbow hits the sky
And God's love carries my problems
like the passing butterfly
I live inside a house of God
His love is like the wood
Providing and protecting
from my problems, He's my Hood
He's the Food that keeps me living
and the Money to survive
As if I was a buzzing bee
He'd be the safely Hive
He's the Radio of knowledge
and the phone's Electric Power
The Ringing of my heartbeat
like that clock rings every hour
There is a space within me
where God sits and fills my soul
Like the single, strongest Battery
in life's remote control.

A MORNING GIFT FROM GOD

A song is sung from heaven
as birds announce the day
And we feel God's presence with us
as we look to Him and pray
With or without problems
our God's forever there
Giving us His guidance
and filling us with care
The day travels on and onward
until the day is night
But with or without sunshine
our God's always our light
We need Him to be with us
just like our need of air
And His comfort does fulfill us
when we're troubled with despair
We gaze up to our Father
when we're confused on what to do
And somehow we find an answer
that is rare, but also true.

GOD'S EYES

God's eyes are felt upon me
as the sun rays hit the land
The sun shines out onto me
I feel touched by the Lord's hand
The light creates a closeness
and the feeling God is near
And knowing God is with me
helps me face nothing with fear
Then white clouds cover the sunlight
until darkness fills the sky
But still without the sunlight
I know God is by my side
I know that He is with me
even though He's not in sight,
'Cause what my eyes just cannot see
they feel with strength and might

ON THE WALKWAY OF LIFE

A light shines down
showing the way
The chosen trail
to travel this day
The road of life
is a path for just one
Laid out by the Lord
unseen by anyone
Streets in the world
toward each here and there
Lanes stretching out
every way, everywhere
Presenting selections
from which we must choose
And the guidance of God
we all need to use
We've each got a path
that we travel with God
We walk not alone
'cause He is our Rod
No matter which route
that we pick to explore
To walk onto it,
God must open the door.

THE ETERNAL CHAMPION

Evil can't conquer
for the Lord is above
To guide and protect
with His spirit of love
His love is the key
in the lock of our lives
As He opens our souls
our goodness will rise
Darkness won't reach us
the light always wins
Forgiveness and love
will stop many sins
Passion has power
the scorn can't subdue
The strength of God's love
just flows through and through
Hatred gets weaker
by each moment of care
And the world is defended
'cause God's everywhere

LET THERE BE LIGHT

Shadows are broken
and darkness does fade
'Cause sun rays come down
and brightness is made
Light from the heavens
and light from the sky
Brighten the world
as we feel God is nigh
There is light in the day
there is light in the night
'Cause the love of the Lord
is more than just bright
Rays from the sun
brighten the street
But it is really God
Who can lift a heartbeat
In total darkness
is how we would be
If the love of the Lord
was not here to see

INVISIBLE, BUT STILL PRESENT

The night is calm
the day is done
Still the eyes of God
are on everyone
Though the world becomes dark
and turns black in the night
The Lord is watching
we're kept in His sight
Often prays are asking
God for His care
But the love of the Lord
is already everywhere
I know He is with me
as the seed of my life
He adds to delight
and crumbles the strife
He surrounds me with comfort
as He touches my soul
He's the force pushing me
getting me to my goal
With me forever
the Lord is around
Invisible or not,
God's name should be crowned

GOD'S LOVE KEEPS ME WARM

The chill from the wind
and the frost in the air
Just doesn't compare
to the cold in my heart
If God wasn't a part
He warms up my body
till my spirit is whole
Tendering my words,
giving heat to my soul
The creation of warmth
in my body and mind
From the love of the Lord
Who is truly divine
It fills me with comfort
and it fills me with peace
Since I am surrounded
with a love that won't cease
And throughout His knowledge
His comfort and care
There's never a problem
that I cannot bare

THE TUNNEL OF LIFE

There's a light at the end of the tunnel
a light that only God gives
It stands as the goal that is reached for
in the burrow of life that we live
It's the gateway to heaven
and the doorway to peace
And a sign from the Lord
that all problems will cease
We each will walk on
one step at a time
And since God is with us
everything turns out fine
We reach for that light
and know the best is to come
'Cause the spirit of God
will fulfill everyone
The walkway is tight
but the Lord is the Light
So we travelers have might
since the Lord's in our sight.

THE STRENGTH OF LOVE

Divinity around me
I feel with my soul
Receiving His love
will always console
I fill up with peace
at the thought of the Lord
He is the Strength
forever adored
There's no time to suffer
for the Lord is so near
Love builds me with boldness
leaving no room for fear
No worries can break through
a heart full of love
Because nothing is stronger,
then the love from above.

THE LORD IS MY PILOT

Smoke is drifting in the night
and God appears
He is my Light
He guides my ways
When I am blind
He looks on earth
And me He finds
He speaks my words
And opens my heart
and all my worries, break apart
He knows the paths,
the roads to take
I follow Him,
make no mistake
He sees my body
and fills my soul
And drives me,
to my lifetime goal.

THE KEY OF LIFE

His Light is shining on me
His love goes through and through
Without the Lord beside me
I don't know what I'd do
A Father He is to me
a Companion and a Friend
I'll never have to worry
God's love has not an end
There's inner strength from knowing
that God is more than near
The touching of His presence
can bring my eye to tear
Spreading His love within me
brings a lifting to my soul
And the power He puts in me
just builds my self-control
I'm under God's protection,
forever will I be
When a lock door blocks the way to peace
the Lord's the only Key.

THE INNER THOUGHTS OF DAVID

(inspiration-David and Goliath, Samuel:23-58)

The power of God is with me
I know what I have to do
I may be small and fragile
but with God, I'll make it through
For God gives me strength
and I feel very strong
Since God is with me
none can go wrong
Looking up I get courage,
looking up I get strength
With God on my side
I can run any length
I can fight any battle,
I can win any race
I can fight to the finish
though I go at slow pace
I am small, I am weak
in the eyes of the world
But the Lord's on my side
and so I've nothing to hide.

THE DIVINE MERCY

(Inspiration: Chaplet Of The Divine Mercy)

For the sake of His sorrowful passion
His mercy descends from above
As we ask Him for pity upon us
we see that it's found in His love
His regard for the world is remarkable
it's concern that's surrounded by peace
The unconditional love that He sends us
is everlasting and will never cease
The heart of the Lord dwells inside us
it fills up each part of the soul
For support we can turn to our Father
and we do it to truly be whole
The Holy Spirit then comes down upon us
to lighten the troubles we face
We atone for the sins of the whole world
and God places upon us His grace
The divinity of God is eternal
holy, mighty, immortal
For compassion we ask,
'cause we know we'll receive
He will give us His mercy
we more than believe.

REMEMBER YOUR BLESSINGS

A world of enigma,
dilemmas, and pain
How many troubles
can a person retain
Some more than others
you can't even bare
The confusion they have
the troubles they wear
You see another person
with more problems than you
So count all your blessings
and then see them through
Think what you have
not what you might need
It could sometimes amount
to a lifetime of greed
Realize your goodness
and where it has been
Know that the Lord
brings it out from within.

JUST ONE BIG FAMILY

(Inspiration: Gen. 4:1-3)

The grass is green
the world's been made
Adam and Eve
began the decade
The creation of families
as generations pass on
Brother to brother
from the night till the dawn
No strangers around
each a relative of me
The closeness of family
I look and I see
The people around me
known or unknown
In a way, are with me
'cause we're from the same bone
To feel close to another,
as if he were by brother,
To sense love in the air
and see people who care
Even more than a friend
every person I see
It's just cousin to cousin
so I feel unity

HE IS MY SAVIOR

The Lord is my Savior
and I have been saved
He brightens my soul
like a street that's been paved
I know that He loves you
and I know He loves me
'Cause He has invited us
to live eternally
And I feel closer to Him
each day that I live
And I know in my heart
if you ask He will give
For the Lord is my Savior,
my Shepherd and King
So forever and always
He'll mean everything

GROWTH FROM GOD

The Lord is our God
caring is His heart
Loving and peaceful
and from Him we won't part
He's the Supreme Being,
holy and humble combined
We've learned through our faith
that our God is Divine
He opens the door
and lets all of us in
When we feel that we'll loose
He helps us to win
The Lord gives us hope
and the help that we need
To live life to the fullest
because He is our Seed.
A flower grows upward
toward the sun up above
Like we grow in our faith
from God and His love

<u>GOD KNOWS THE WAY</u>

Touched by God and all His grace
are the people of this earthly place
Nothing compares to God's bright shine
He is the maker, only He is Divine
God's love is the breeze
that flows through the day
We live through our lives
while He leads the way
His unseen footprints mark the ground
and point the way to peace,
But never ever will there be
a time His love does cease
We'll come to an intersection
while God walks us through our life
And choose the right path to take
when accepting His advice
So we follow the Lord,
'cause He knows the way
We'll never get lost,
we'll conquer the day

GOD'S CHILDREN

Each living thing
is a child of God
No one is alone
to face what is hard
I am just not alone
'cause all people are here
To be children of God
for God comforts each tear
Shining in heaven
God paints all the Earth
With a glow on the land
when there will be a birth
There's a feeling of passion
when God is in mind
He knows of the warmth
and the peace that He'll find
Watching His children
all day and all night
With a heart of His love
that is constantly bright
The Lord is a parent
to each living thing
And a feeling of value
is what He does bring

GOD CONQUERS ALL

At first it was near
but now it is here
The trouble is big
but with God there's no fear
He knows when we're happy
He knows when we're said
He simply sees all
the good and the bad
Since His love bring us comfort
we can, the problem face
His love is abundant
and it fills us with grace
He helps us to realize
what is needed to know
That facing dilemmas
brings boldness to grow
God aids us with spirit
to deal with our strife
As God conquers all,
in the headaches of life

FAITH IS SIGHT

I don't have to see God
to know He is there
I don't have to touch Him
to feel all His care
My closeness to God
brings His sight to my mind
And knowing He's there
just tightens our bind
My mind is what sees Him
as He touches my soul
He's not ever viewed
yet His presence is bold
I trust He is with me,
it is what I believe
I don't need to question,
"Would He ever leave"
He inspires my soul
in my mind, He's my goal
He's not only one part,
He is my whole heart.

THE HANDS OF GOD

Raping His arms around you,
touching you with His hand
The bond He makes is tight
as tight as a stretched band
His hands reach out to grasp you
and cuddle you in His arms
He tells you, "You are safe"
and blocks you from all harm
He takes the loads inside you
and carries every one
He sees troubles in the world
and wants you to have none
Our God and His ten fingers
they point the way to go
And you follow His suggestion,
'cause, what to do you know He knows
The palms of God are full
of His children everywhere
He holds and never drops
because He's full of love and care

<u>MY SYMBOL OF HOPE</u>

My heart feels dark,
my soul feels weak
I'm looking to God
it's Him that I seek
I need Him to help me
and fill me with peace
To calm all my hurting
till my trouble does cease
I turn to my Father,
I reach for His care
I know that with Him
all my problems, I'll bare
He will fill me with hope
and finally I'll cope
To fix what has broken
the Lord is my token.

LORD, LEND ME YOUR HAND

Weaker and weaker
unable to stand
Please show me the way
just lend me Your hand
Pull me the right way
with You, I won't fall
Escort me and guide me
up and over each wall
Lord, when I'm lost
and no one's around
Lend me Your hand
and I will be found
When I'm in trouble
if I know that You're there
The help that You'll give
will be a breath of fresh air
If I slip or I mess up
I'll reach out to You
Because with Your hand
I've no doubt what to do

LET GOD BE YOUR HELP

When your spirit reaches down below
and you find your strength is gone
Look to God our Father,
'cause with Him you're not forlorn
Let not your heart be troubled
in your presence He is there
He'll help you solve the puzzles
and problems you can't bare.
If you are feeling sorrow,
sadness, pain or grief
With each day and each tomorrow
God will fill you with relief
A remedy for heartache
is the love for God you feel
And as you think of our God
it's as if your problems heal
Challenges you're dealt with
upsetting as they be
the Lord is there to help you
So you feel not stressed, but free.

I send a large debt of gratitude to my College English Professor **Gian DiDonna** and my mother, **Barbara Regan**.

Thank You

A smile to cherish
for it's lift of the day
A friend who convinces
a sinner to pray
The clapping of hands
or the wink of an eye
Will be gleaming and glowing
like a star in the sky
A heart that keeps beating,
in a friend who stays true,
My gratitude and thanks
is given to you.

About The Author

Only The Thought Of Helplessness, was a part of **Leanora Marie Regan's** life when she was eleven, while most children were enjoying life and emotionally stable. She has graduated college with a Bachelors Degree in English literature and writing. She is living with her mother, father and brother. In addition, she has three cats and a dog (even though she's allergic to them). She has many friends, and knows each one is a gift from God.